'Paul Delaney g͟͟͟͟͟͟͟͟͟͟͟͟͟͟͟͟͟͟͟͟͟͟͟͟d on and on and on and on and on and on and on and on and on and on and on and on and on and on and on and on and on and on and on and on!'
(Anon)

www.pdelaney.co.uk

First published in September 2016 by FeedARead.com

Second edition published February 2017

Text © Paul Delaney

Cover illustrations © Christine Enright

Design © The Pig tourist publishing

The author and illustrator assert their moral right under the Copyright, Designs and Patents Act, 1988, to be identified as the author and illustrator of this work.

All Rights reserved. No part of this publication may be reproduced, copied, stored in a retrieval system, or transmitted, in any form or by any means, without the prior written consent of the copyright holder, nor be otherwise circulated in any form of binding or cover other than that in which it is published and without a similar condition being imposed on the subsequent purchaser.

A CIP catalogue record for this title is available from the British Library.

Other books by Paul Delaney:

(All available in paperback / kindle download)

Sparrowlegs

I'm fed up! (poetry)

My toilet is a murderer!

The Magical Madame Mistral

Hedgehogs 1 Big trucks 0 (poetry)

Coming soon –

Norris Snoot

Lionheart

Y6 'Author of the month – Paul Delaney' display at
**Penketh South Primary School,
Warrington, Cheshire, England.**

One of the happiest schools I've ever worked in!

Paul Delaney is a poet, a writer and a professional organist. He spends his time writing stories and poems and playing the organ and piano. Recently, Paul has founded successful school poetry festivals, developing children's love of both writing and performing their own modern poetry.

Paul enjoys visiting schools across the U.K. and beyond, conducting creative writing workshops.
However, he's now in great demand as a school dinner tester. Paul's 'Most scrumptious school dinners in the world' award is currently held by Knightsbridge School, London, England.

Paul has three cool and trendy boys called Harry, George and Freddie. They're all super sporty too but Paul wasn't. He played winger once in a Rugby Union match and didn't touch the ball once. So he took up 'Snakes and ladders' instead.

www.pdelaney.co.uk

An accomplished artist and illustrator, Christine Enright studied illustration at Manchester Metropolitan University. Christine works in a variety of styles and media and is an accomplished portrait painter. Christine's first published children's book was 'Darkly Demon' by DM Lever and published by Electric press.

In addition to her own commissions, Christine is now having fun working with talented children's authors, especially Paul Delaney as they went to the same primary school in Widnes, Cheshire.

Christine is married with two grown up children. Whilst painting, she enjoys drinking mugs of tea and last week, went through 267 tea bags.

www.facebook.com/ChristineEnrightArtist

For Mum and Dad

'The lunatic, the lover and the poet
are of imagination all compact.'

A Midsummer Night's Dream
William Shakespeare
1595

With special thanks to:

Tina Richardson-Hignett, Y6 teacher and English language expert extraordinaire.

Kimiya Hickling, Tamzin Burnip and Hollie Houghton from Rāwhiti School, Christchurch, New Zealand for their superb pencil illustrations!

My favourite trainers

Paul Delaney

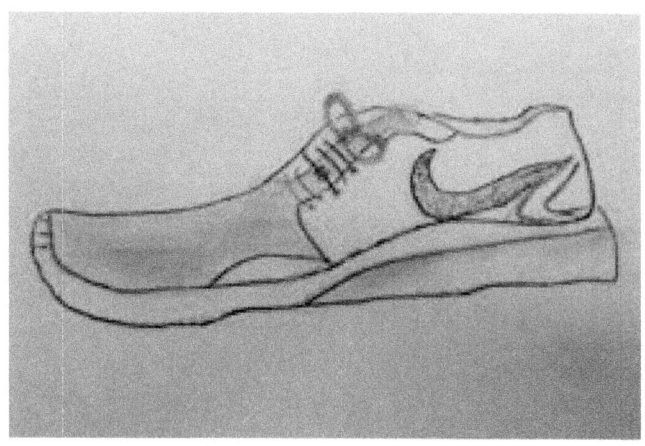

Picture: Tamzin Burnip, Rāwhiti School, New Zealand

'Yes, I am a dreamer. For a dreamer is one who can only find his way by moonlight and his punishment is this – he sees the dawn before the rest of the world...'

Oscar Wilde (1854 – 1900)

My favourite trainers

I placed my favourite trainers today,
into some charity bags.
It only seems like yesterday,
pulling off their tags.

They've travelled with me for countless miles,
in all sorts of weather,
treading through my ups and downs
and wearing out their leather.

As I dropped them into their humble abodes,
I said a little prayer.
Somebody, somewhere would use them,
despite their wear and tear.

An African teenager on the plains perhaps,
impressing his favourite girl;
or an Indian princess pauper,
giving them a whirl.

I placed the enormous bags outside
and waited for the van.
Tears poured forth from my bulging eyes
as I spotted the collection man.

I closed my door and sprinted upstairs,
dropping onto my King Size bed.
I buried my head into my pillow
and this is what I said:

*'May the soles of the faithful departed,
through the mercy of God, rest in peace. Amen.'*

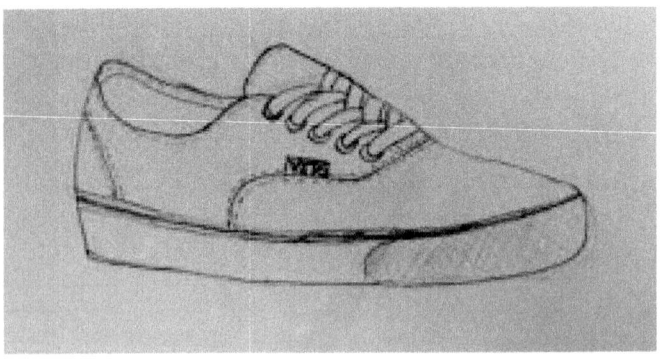

Kimiya Hickling, Rāwhiti School, New Zealand

Two childhood jigsaws

A week or so later,
a different bag was pushed through my door.
'Save the earth,' the label read,
but I'd seen it all before.

I found an old scarf, a broken watch
and a pair of football socks.
And two jigsaw puzzles, their pieces still sitting,
in a faded, cardboard box.

The van arrived promptly, the very next day,
a battered but loveable Ford.
A man in overalls clambered out,
grabbing his brand new load.

I thought of my jigsaws I'd given away
as I'd played with them as a child.
And again it happened, I was swamped with
regret and I wanted to run and hide.

Jigsaw One was Concorde's cockpit,
a difficult puzzle to complete.
Jigsaw Two was a herd of camels,
basking in the heat.

I closed my door and sprinted upstairs,
dropping onto my King Size bed.
I buried my head into my pillow
and this is what I said:

*'Dear Lord, I loved those jigsaws dearly.
So may they rest in pieces. Amen'*

Miss Campbell's SWEET revenge!

Miss Campbell the dentist sat in her chair,
in her cramped, uninviting room.
A patient appeared and sat in *her* chair,
confronting her appointment with doom.

'I know that face,' Miss Campbell whispered,
tugging her assistant's sleeve.
'The things she did to me at school,
nobody would believe.'

'Well get your revenge,' the assistant remarked,
passing Miss Campbell the drill.
'Pretend a healthy molar's
in need of an immediate fill.'

'She made my life hell,' Miss Campbell whispered.
'Nobody will understand it fully.
I hated school and failed my exams,
all because of this bully.'

'An eye for an eye,' her assistant said.
'And a tooth for a tooth so they say!
Pardon the pun but revenge is sweet,
so it's time to make her pay!'

'Open wide,' Miss. Campbell said,
lowering her victim's chair.
She drew the drill to the bully's mouth
and into her eyes did stare.

'There's a tooth at the back, it's rotten and black,
too much sugar's probably to blame.'
And she turned the dial on her silver drill
to maximum bleeding and pain!

SWEET REVENGE!

The tragic and cruel life of a teabag

Pulled out from its cardboard box,
I suppose it's destiny.
Dropped into a favourite mug,
to make a cup of tea.

Boiled alive for several minutes.
Tortured by a spoon.
Squashed to the brink of death like a traitor.
Cruel, horrific wounds.

Tossed aside, onto a plate.
Left in the cold to die.
Scraped into a silver bin.
A haunting, weakening cry.

A final breath, in that trash,
on the top of a rotting meat pie.
The teabag spirit breathes its last
and escapes into the sky.

There is no funeral or memorial service.
There is no grave to see.
So next time you choose a teabag,
choose it carefully…

Seven supermarket trolleys

Look at her over there,
with a lettuce in her trolley.
She must be on a diet
if she likes that sort of stuff.
It's her new year's resolution
and it's probably a folly.
Her meal-deal's a carrot
and a sandwich filled with fluff.

Look at him over there,
with cans of Coke in his trolley.
He's asking for trouble,
if he drinks that sort of stuff.
It's a dentist's nightmare
as it's loaded with sugar.
But toothpaste and mouthwash
should be enough.

Look at her over there,
with tins of dog food in her trolley.
She must be loaded
if she buys that sort of stuff.
It's the most expensive brand,
far too good for her hound.
But perhaps it's for her
and her language is 'woof, woof!'

Look at her over there,
with sirloin steaks in her trolley.
She's not a vegetarian,
if she likes that sort of stuff.
She could be a competitor on
'Come dine with me!'
But grill those steaks too long
and they'll turn out tough.

Look at her over there,
with porridge oats in her trolley.
She's obviously a health freak
if she likes that sort of stuff.
She's believes all that hype
about whole grain oats.
But I'd rather fill my bowl
with sugar coated puffs.

Look at him over there,
with twelve roses in his trolley.
He's hopelessly in love,
if he buys that sort of stuff.
Perhaps he's saying sorry
for upsetting his wife,
patching up a marriage
all broken and duff.

Look at her over there
with her son in her trolley.
She's not risk assessing,
if she does that sort of stuff.
He's sitting on the panel
of the self-service checkout.
So the weighing computer
exclaims with a gruff:

'Unexpected toddler in bagging area!'

Arrgghh!

The invisible fisherman

Whatever's happened to the fish in our pond?
They've sort of disappeared.
Dad thinks next-door's cat's responsible.
'If I could get my hands on that
MONSTROUS moggy...'

Mum thinks the culprit's a giant frog.
'As if frogs eat fish, Mum!' I shout.
'You've seen River Monsters, haven't you?'
Mum answers, shooting out a wry smile.
'You know - that programme on TV.'

'But our fish are massive,' I reply.
'Anyway, I don't think frogs eat fish!'
'It could be that hedgehog that visits,'
my little sister says.

'Don't be daft, Isabella,' I cry.
'A hedgehog will just sink to the bottom.'
'I reckon it's a fisherman,' Grandad says,
folding his arms tight. 'Trust me, I know.'

Everybody giggles.
'Time for school,' Dad says.
We all scatter from the table.
'Brush your teeth you two,' Mum says.

I climb the stairs, obeying Mum's command.
Then I stare out of my bedroom window.
I wait, my eyes peering into the pond.

It appears from nowhere, a long, silver lance,
striking the water at an incredible speed.
The creature emerges from the water.
A dancing, golden fish is trapped,
caught in this powerful predator's beak.

The heron's huge wings cut through the air, flapping gracefully. Disappearing from sight, this majestic bird heads for home, its warm nest hidden in a secret, shadowy place, perched high in an unknown tree.

'Come on Jack!' Dad shouts.
'You'll be late for school.'
'I know what's eating our fish!' I exclaim.
Dad staresat me. 'What?'
'A Great Blue Heron!'

'There's never been any herons around here for
years, Son,' Dad says.
'They're an endangered species I think.'

It's pointless arguing. Dad's always right.
Well he *thinks he's* right.
But this time he's wrong.

'I told you it was a fisherman, didn't I?' Grandad
whispers, his lips cracking into a broad smile.
'That Great Blue Heron's been around for years.
But always remember this, Jack:

Some people will never believe anything
out of the ordinary. Nothing at all.

Unless they see it with their own eyes.'

'I think you're right, Grandad…'

Life is strange

Life is strange with its twists and turns.
Our human face giggles and gurns.

Lonely we travel, down these roads,
carrying our backpacks and heavy loads.

Of tremors and troubles and days to forget
and painful memories and decisions to regret.

But then we meet somebody;
Serendipity calls!

And love changes everything,
breaking down walls.

And life is never quite the same again…

* Serendipity: The occurrence and development of events by 'chance' in a happy, beneficial way.

Four imaginary walls

I stare north and see a brick wall.
I stare east and see a brick wall.
I stare south and see a brick wall.
I stare west and see a brick wall.

Imaginary walls, created by my mind.
I close my eyes.
I haul in a deep pocket of air.
I puff out a long breath.

And then I smile.
In the corner of my prison's illusion,
there lies something - a sledgehammer.

The door in the corner

'We've had a wonderful time over the years,
the children growing up and laughter and tears.
We've travelled together, my very best friend,
down winding paths and twisting bends.
But now it's time to go…

We've sprinted through fields and caravan sites
and played on the sands, chasing colourful kites.
We've pushed through streams, netting silver fishes
and weaved our magical, golden wishes.
But now, it's time to go…

We've trudged through forests, side by side,
when life was tough and I wanted to hide.
I'd lost all hope, drowning in drink
but your sparkling eyes stopped me to think.
But now it's time to go…

We've climbed up mountains, scaling the heights
and reached their summits and breathtaking sights.
We've weathered life's storms, rowing our boat
and somehow managed to stay afloat.
But now it's time to go…

We've laughed and joked, living life's dream,
supporting each other like a prize-winning team.
We've enjoyed a drink, down at the pub,
warmed by the fire on that old, patterned rug,
But now it's time to go...'

'Come on, then Oscar,' the old man sighed,
dragging a tissue over sunken eyes.
He led his companion towards a door,
shuffling his feet across the floor.
As now it's time to go...

A girl appeared, all dressed in white,
a poignant prelude to a heavenly flight.
The old dog stared into his master's eyes,
licking his hand, their final goodbye.
As now it's time to go...

The angel in white took the old dog's lead
and the man dropped down, onto his knees.
He ruffled his best friend's face and ears,
whispering thanks whilst spluttering tears.

As the door in the corner opened...

A bird with a broken wing

I discovered a bird today,
a bird with a broken wing.

Pain and shock was invading his body,
but he continued to sing.

He fluttered his shattered feathers,
desperately trying to fly.

But in my hands his spirit was fading
as he dreamed of flying high.

Perhaps he flew into a lamppost.
Perhaps he flew into a tree.

Perhaps a tomcat pounced on him,
hungry for his tea.

Perhaps he crashed into a windscreen,
a car travelling too fast.

But in my hands, he gazed into my eyes
and then he breathed his last.

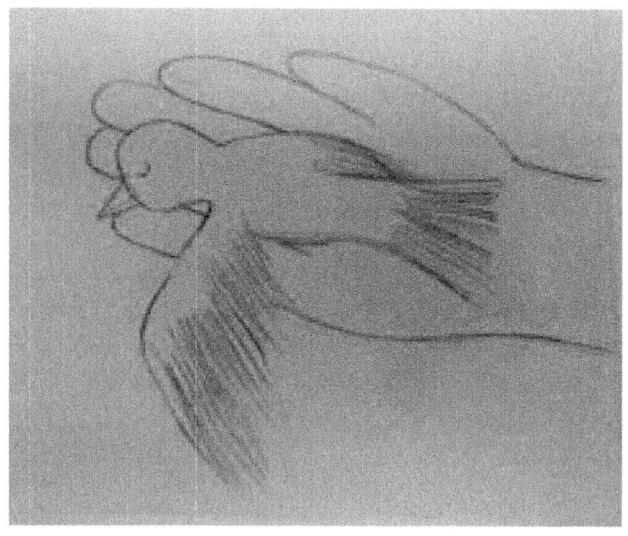

Hollie Houghton, Rāwhiti School, New Zealand

Ripples in a pond

A wizard tossed a precious pebble,
into a mystical pond.
A ripple appeared as he chanted his words,
waving a wooden wand.

He stroked his beard, muttering a verse,
conjuring up a spell.
And through the trees, a whisper came,
accompanied by a bell.

'What do you seek?' a Master asked.
'What do you want of me?'
'Tell me my future,' the wizard cried.
'Tell me what you see.'

*'I see a wild and vicious, howling hound,
strangling your soul.
I see its grinding, crunching silver teeth,
gnawing at your whole.*

*I see its evil eyes, lighting up,
like coals in caverns of darkness.
I see its misty, smothering shadow,
extinguishing your brightness.*

'What else do you see?'

*'I see a shivering, shining star,
landing at your feet.
I see its fragile brightness,
battling against defeat.*

*I see it permeate your entirety,
a light of eternal love.
I see its beauty, above the horizon,
in the heavenly vaults above.*

'Which one will grow?' the wizard asked.
'If you know, please shout it out.'
'The one you feed,' the Master replied.
'Of that, I have no doubt.'

The staffroom of broken dreams

What happens in the staffroom? I don't really know.
Children are forbidden; they're not allowed to go

through that door, where teachers talk
and angels sing but devils walk.

They're huddled in groups, tuning into the news,
sipping their coffee and expressing their views.

Wild, withered witches, gathered in throngs,
composing laments about education's wrongs.

Dreaming of the lifestyle! What a 'Lotto' win brings!
But ripping up their tickets and broken wings.

Old Mrs Hall sits in the corner,
chatting to a student, trying to warn her.
'Run away Abigail, I can see it in your eyes.
Don't follow my footsteps to a job you despise.'

Sporty Mr Benn sits next to Mrs Hall,
wearing a tracksuit and clutching a ball.
'I once played for England's under eighteens
but a terrible tackle ended my dreams.'

Slim Mrs Moon sits next to Mr Benn,
marking her books with a ballpoint pen.
*'I once danced in pantomimes, the Queen of the stage
but my lucky break eluded me; I waited for an age.'*

Big Mrs Foy sits next to Mrs Moon,
doing her impression of a hot air balloon.
*'I once was a supermodel, as thin as a rake
until I discovered chocolate and cake.'*

Young Mr Grice sits next to Mrs Foy,
staring at the screen on his brand new toy.
*'I was going to be a doctor but I flunked my final tests,
so I ended up in class, teaching nuisances and pests.*

Happy Miss Molloy sits next to Mr Grice,
planning a lesson using seven-sided dice.
*'I LOVE my job so much, you just wouldn't believe!
If you're a moaner or a groaner, then...*

Why don't you leave?

A load of words

You can **unload** a wardrobe,
an IKEA flat pack.
You can **upload** a photograph,
onto your Mac.

You can **offload** a rugby ball,
whilst a player's on your back.
You can **download** 'Thriller',
Michael Jackson's classic track.

You can **overload** your mind
but you'll probably crack.
As an invisible sledgehammer
strikes your head – whack!

You can **explode** a stick of dynamite
but it's wrong in a spelling test.
I've exhausted all the 'load' words,
so I'm going for a rest!

A serendipitous dog walk

Marching across a muddy field,
an old man and hound
trot together silently,
a symbol of laughter and love.

A lonely widower's canine;
A faithful friend is found.
Jigsaw pieces fitting together,
hands in knitted gloves.

Every morning at eight o'clock,
Tommy pulls the lead
from a hook on the back of the kitchen door,
an inconspicuous place.

Sam the spaniel spins and leaps,
a lovable, playful breed.
And happiness fills his master's bones,
spreading to his face.

Through the park they trot together,
man and his very best friend.
A treasure trove of unconditional love;
A wondrous, heavenly walk.

A terrier appears with a lonely old lady
and a broken heart to mend.
Sam the spaniel sniffs the terrier
and their owners start to talk.

Dogs dash, sprint and chase;
Spirits young and free.
One old man and a lonely lady,
walking their dogs on the grass.

They did not know each other before.
Love's blind so they couldn't see.
But now their journey's about to begin
and happiness will come to pass.

Johnny Johnson's lone Spitfire

On the bottom of the English Channel;
lies a rusting, wrecked Spitfire.
Squadron leader Johnny Johnson's
still strapped in its cockpit's seat.
A handsome chap in those halcyon days,
a renowned and excellent flyer.
Brought down by the guns of a German ace,
a dashing, formidable feat.

Still tucked inside Johnny's pocket,
below his pilot's wings,
is an old, damp photograph,
of his fiancée, Charlotte Wright.
A blushing and beautiful English rose.
Oh the pleasures true love brings!
But Charlotte's heart was broken forever,
on that cruel, summer's night.

On the bottom of the English Channel,
lies a mangled Messerschmitt.
Oberleutnant Erich Hauptmann's
still strapped in its cockpit's seat.
A brave warrior, tall and blonde,
who possessed an inventive wit.
Brought down by the guns of an English ace,
an untimely, cruel exit.

Still tucked inside Erich's pocket,
sat below his eagle's wings,
is an old, damp photograph,
of his fiancée, Lara Faust.
Childhood sweethearts, hopelessly in love,
two sweet and innocent things.
But Lara's heart was broken forever,
on the night of that aerial jaust.

I suppose I'll never know!

Look at him over there, with the black, bushy beard,
thinking he's trendy when really he's weird.

Why would you want a ring through your nose,
tattoos on your arms and fingers and toes?

Why would you want to wear that shirt,
wobbling like a penguin and looking like a Blurt?

I suppose I'll never know…

Look at her over there, with the shocking pink locks,
stomping in her bovver boots and long, stripy socks.

Why would you want a dress like that,
when you're not even slim, you're incredibly fat?

Why would you want to look like a ghoul,
attracting negativity but thinking you're cool?

I suppose I'll never know…

Look at him over there, with the big fat belly,
wobbling around like an enormous jelly.

Why would you want a shaved hairstyle,
looking like an extra from Jeremy Kyle?

Why would you want your fingers full of rings,
dripping in gold, like Pharaohs and Kings?

I suppose I'll never know...

Look at her over there, with the jewel in her nose,
dragging on a cigarette, polluting her clothes.

Why would you want to inhale that stuff,
when factory smoke is probably enough?

Why would you want to spend all your cash,
on lethal toxins and volcanic ash?

I suppose I'll never know...
Look at me, over here, courting poisonous lovers,
judging sacred books by their colourful covers.

Why would I want to treat people like that?
When my own life's a tyre all punctured and flat.

Why would I want to criticise strangers,
reflections of Jesus, lying in mangers.
I suppose I'll never know...

Why not?

'Where's your homework?' Mr Webster asked,
invading Rosie's space, his voice an icy blast.
'You're constantly yawning and your eyes are all red.
So what unearthly hour are you crawling into bed?'

My mum's very ill, Rosie Richards thought,
her eyes all heavy and glazed.
*And I'm her full time carer,
so I think you'll be amazed*

*at the stuff I do every day,
like washing her greying hair.
And looking in her fitted wardrobe
for her favourite clothes to wear.*

*And getting her breakfast ready,
like hot, buttered toast.
And smoothing on her make up,
a clown or ghoulish ghost.*

*And sorting out her daily tablets,
medicines large and small.
And welcoming doctors and nurses
into our lounge and hall.*

'Where's your homework?' Mr Webster asked,
invading Rosie's space, his voice an icy blast.
'You're constantly yawning and your eyes are all red.
So what unearthly hour are you crawling into bed?'

My mum's very ill, Rosie Richards thought,
her eyes all heavy and glazed.
*And I'm her full time carer,
so I think you'll be amazed*

*at the stuff I do every day,
little things folk never see.
Like pushing mum into the toilet,
maintaining her dignity.*

*And pushing a bulging trolley
around a supermarket store.
And cleaning up my mummy's sick
from the cold, kitchen floor.*

*And collecting doctors' prescriptions
from the pharmacy in the town.
And making mummy a cup of tea
when she's all fed up and down.*

'Where's your homework?' Mr Webster asked,
invading Rosie's space, his voice an icy blast.
'You're constantly yawning and your eyes are all red.
So what unearthly hour are you crawling into bed?'

My mum's very ill, Rosie Richards thought,
her eyes all heavy and glazed.
And I'm her full time carer,
so I think you'll be amazed

at the stuff I do every day,
like having our grown up talks.
And tucking my mum into bed at night,
for dreams of countryside walks.

And watching all my friends walk past,
on their way to the boys in the park.
And hearing them scream with laughter,
sprinting past my house after dark.

And looking at posts on Instagram
of normal teenage things.
And feeling life's just shattered dreams,
like birds with broken wings.

'Where's your homework?' Mr Webster asked,
invading Rosie's space, his voice an icy blast.
'You're constantly yawning and your eyes are all red.
So what unearthly hour are you crawling into bed?'

'Sorry, Sir, I haven't done it.'

'WHY NOT?'

Menagerie minds

An Eagle's voice, a devilish voice,
a burden as heavy as a boulder:
'I'll steal away, steal away,
steal your dreams away.'

A Kingfisher's voice, an angel's voice,
a friend resting on my shoulder:
'Just make a wish, make a wish,
make a wonderful wish.'

So many characters in our heads,
fluttering their wings like birds.
All power and strength, a continual struggle,
like greedy, gluttonous Lairds.

A Vulture's voice, a witch's voice,
a grandma's face but older.
'It'll never work, never work,
never ever work.'

A Robin's voice, a spirit's voice,
a burning ember a smoulder.
'Believe in yourself, believe in yourself,
really, really believe.'

So many characters in our heads,
fluttering their wings like birds.
All power and strength, a continual struggle,
like greedy, gluttonous Lairds.

A Magpie's voice, a Snow Queen's voice,
a sharp shard of ice but colder.
'You're going to fail, you're going to fail,
you're obviously going to fail.'

A wise owl's voice, a sergeant's voice,
a battle hardened soldier.
'Remember the words of Winston Churchill –
'Never, ever QUIT!'

Voices gallop across our minds
like wild, buffalo herds.
Black and white personality throngs.
A menagerie of different birds.

Sorrowful songs and melancholy moods,
collections of poisonous words.
Happy harmonies of sweet sounding chords.
Minor sixths and major thirds.

So many characters in our heads,
fluttering their wings like birds.
All power and strength, a continual struggle,
like greedy, gluttonous Lairds.

A definition of clauses

Independent clause (Main clause):

I like Aimee's friend.

Dependent clause (Subordinate clause)

I like Aimee's friend *even though she's annoying!*

Relative clause

I like Aimee's friend, *who is called Sadie,* even though she is annoying!

Santa Claus

A big, jolly man who often goes by the name of 'Father Christmas' and works one day a year.

Cat's clause

Curved and pointed horny nails on each digit of the feet of a cat. *Or is it Cat's claws?*

Father Michael's favourite dish

I asked Father Michael,
what is your favourite dish?
If you were condemned,
what would be your wish?

The old priest stared
and scratched his head.
He gathered his thoughts
and this is what he said:

'I don't like foreign foods
as they make me rather sick.
It's those herbs and spices.
They have a sort of kick!

You can't beat traditionals,
like beans on toast
or fish, chips and peas
or a Sunday roast.

You can't beat old favourites,
like bacon and egg
or salads in the summer
or meat and two veg.

You can't beat Chef's specials,
like steak and ale pies
or gourmet burgers,
with salad and fries.

You can't beat homemade,
like corned beef hash.
But my favourite dish of all is…

BANGERS AND MASS!

I love your BEAUTIFUL mind

In they wander, a host of loving couples.
One of them walks but the other one shuffles.
Wives and husbands devoid of kerfuffles,
leading their spouses across the room.

A husband chats about the latest news.
A wife pipes up, expressing her views.
Their partners gaze like silent statues
sitting on the surface of a darkened moon.

The atmosphere's pierced by two empty eyes.
A summer sun smothered by thick, cloudy skies.
And who sits next door? A saint in disguise,
a constant carer, an eternal flame of love.

A life full of words - 'In sickness and in health'.
A selfless act of love and spiritual wealth.
A public expression, not secrecy and stealth,
heading down cruel and twisting paths.

A wonderful woman with an empty mind.
A marvellous man. Why is life so unkind?
Wives and husbands and a contract signed
of love and devotion and continuous care.

A photograph album of holidays in Wales.
A sparkle in their eyes and wind in their sails.
Memories awake! Let's remember those tales
of a beautiful life spent together!

A golden, true love is present in that room.
It permeates the air and cuts through the gloom.
One half of those couples is locked in a tomb
but their partners' spirits shine on and on.

'We remember special times, we spent together.
Sitting in our caravans in unpredictable weather.
Raising our children - all birds of a feather
and a life full of happiness and memorable days.

Our journeys together have not yet ceased.
Just one was attacked by a mind-eating beast.
But our love for each other has never decreased
and that's why we remain, together as one.

You're my best friend and I love you. I always will.
You're my almond blossom and I miss you still.
I will never forget the excitement and thrill
of halcyon days and spending my time with you.

I love you x

And I love your beautiful mind xxx

For John and Irene Hatton (RIP)

And St Helens Alzheimer's Society x

Mrs Flossop's date with destiny

Katie Flossop went to the toilet
on an enormous jumbo jet.
She was absolutely bursting,
her knickers almost wet.

'Where do I relieve myself?'
she asked a stewardess.
'I believe I feel a dribble
and this is my favourite dress.'

'It's that big door, over there,'
said the stewardess with a smile.
So Katie Flossop stumbled on,
strolling down the aisle.

Her old ears didn't seem to work
over the jet engines' roar.
So she walked not right but left,
to the emergency exit door.

She grabbed the heavy handle
and pulled it with a yank.
And the big door opened,
with a swish and sudden clank.

Icy air rushed into the cabin
and the passengers were enraged.
Mrs Flossop shouted out:
'This toilet's not engaged!

But it's freezing in this cubicle.
And it's colder than the poles!
I hope this airline does provide,
soft three ply toilet rolls.

I've got a first class ticket
so this shouldn't be allowed!'
She stepped through the emergency door
plunging into cumulus cloud.

'Arrgghh!' she yelled, twisting her legs
as she dropped like a heavy boulder.
She plunged through 30,000 feet,
damp and wet and colder.

She crash-landed with a bang
onto a children's trampoline.
And tossed like a pancake,
a bouncy ball machine.

'What happened?' Katie Flossop asked
as her brain turned to cabbage.
'At least I've missed those airport queues,
waiting for my baggage.

I was bursting for the toilet
but I don't need it any more.
And I do remember something
about falling from a door.'

'You sort of fell from the sky,'
said an orphan with her friend.
'I've been praying for a mother,
for years and years on end.

I've yearned to have a mummy
and feel a daddy's touch.
I've prayed for a real family,
I'm not asking very much!'

Katie's heart was melted
and she hugged this little girl.
She arched her eyes towards the sky,
her mind a hazy whirl.

'My husband and I wanted children,
for many, many years.
But it never, ever happened,
so we focussed on careers.'

'Will you take me home with you?'
asked the girl, twirling her hair.
'My name's Suzanne and Sam's my brother,
that's him just over there.

I think you have a form to fill
and just wait a month or so.
Then if you're a suitable candidate,
the office lets you know.

Mrs Flossop looked at Suzanne
and stared at her brother.
*'I wonder what did happen
to their father and their mother?'*

'I think my mind's made up,' she said
as sunlight lit her face.
'I tumbled through the sky
for a reason, by God's grace.'

She clutched Suzanne's little hands
and Sam's, her young sibling.
And walked towards the office,
to do the decent thing.

Katie Flossop signed the forms
and three long months went by.
She reflected on her 'happy accident'
falling through the sky.

She arrived with her husband,
at the orphanage after tea.
And took two lonely children home
and made a family.

*Sometimes, wonderful things do literally
'drop out of the sky'...*

People

People are the strangest creatures,
including my friends and me.
Take a walk through towns and cities,
it's not that difficult to see.

Skin and bones and hearts and minds,
clinging to a soul.
I suppose we're all the same in essence,
spirits young and old.

'What's life for? Why am I here?'
I hear you stop and say.
Life's a collection of sun and storms.
A typical Shakespeare play.

Everyone's travelling on their road,
towards that heavenly light.
It's dim when you're young but soon you're old,
and suddenly it's bright.

Our children's beautiful toys

Harry's favourite cuddly toys,
well, to be honest, he's got a few.
There's Zigbee, Bungeon and Scarf,
a loveable, furry crew.

George's favourite is a duck called Panny
and a dog called Creamy too.
He's also got Gerrard and Torres
and a Gorilla from the zoo.

Freddie has a Jellycat turtle,
whose name is Turty Tom.
There's Lemon, Wilbur and Barney,
a nightly 'cuddlethon'.

Our children's beautiful toys.
O what happy sunlight beams!
Priceless little treasures,
sharing children's dreams.

Goodnight my little angels,
fly off into the night.
And may your spirits wander,
as free as birds in flight.

Thank you for...

Thank you for a thick, warm sunbeam,
gently caressing my face.
Thank you for a silver star,
mysteriously twinkling in space.

Thank you for a floating snowflake,
drifting in the sky.
Thank you for a snow capped mountain,
stretching up so high.

Close your eyes.
Draw in a deep, life-giving breath.
And in the silence, give thanks.

Thank you for a colourful flower,
swaying quietly in the breeze.
Thank you for its potent perfume,
attracting busy bees.

Thank you for a precious raindrop,
long awaited by desert sands.
Thank you for a wealth of creatures,
unique to different lands.

Close your eyes.
Draw in a deep, life-giving breath.
And in the silence, give thanks.

Thank you for the seas and oceans,
their secrets cold and deep.
Thank you for the seeds of creation,
sowing in order to reap.

Thank you for a carpet of grass,
a field of emerald green.
Thank you for heaven and earth
and the mystery in between.

Close your eyes.
Draw in a deep, life-giving breath.
And in the silence, give thanks.

Thank you for a forest of trees,
damp jungles and ancient woods.
Thank you for a puddle to stamp in,
left by ruthless floods.

Thank you for my spirit's essence,
as I am truly unique.
Thank you for the answers
to the secrets that I seek.

Close your eyes.
Draw in a deep, life-giving breath.
And in the silence, give thanks.

For if we appreciate

ALL that's around us,

it's good to be alive...

A frog saw his love

A frog saw his love, resting on a rock.
She was sitting in the middle of a pond,
cold and all alone.

The frog couldn't swim properly.
The rock far, far away.

So he waited around to pluck up courage
on another, distant day.

A frog saw his love, resting on a rock.
She was chatting to a bullfrog,
Flirting the hours away.

The frog couldn't swim properly.
The rock far, far away.

So he waited around to pluck up courage,
on another, distant day.

A frog saw a rock, a sculpture in a pond.
The rock seemed deserted,
a cold and lonely place,

The frog couldn't swim properly.
The rock far, far away.

But his love had disappeared
to plan her wedding day...

I blame myself

Every time I see her,
my heart is captivated.
My brain is breaking down,
like vintage cheddar grated.
I should have asked her out back then
but I procrastinated.
So even though I talk to her,
we've never ever dated.

I'd say she is my number one,
if she was ever rated.
Her name is on my wish list,
at its summit situated.
I should have been proactive
but I just simply waited.
But nothing ever happened
so my destiny created.

I see her now and then
and my mood it gets deflated.
I think of all those years ago,
this special girl I feted.
I didn't say 'I love you' so
perhaps I should have baited.
But now it doesn't matter,
as it's all a bit belated.

'She is always on my mind'
as that famous ballad stated.
But I will never forget her,
the girl I should have mated.
I still see her fabled features
and briefly I'm elated.
But now, alone, I blame myself,
a being so berated.

St Michael's View

A jobless girl lives in Flat number two.
She might be single but I don't have a clue.

Sometimes I can hear her haunting cries
and I see her pain in her bloodshot eyes.

She walks past me not saying a word,
her mind still fizzing and her vision blurred.

A very young mum lives in Flat number four.
She's new on the block; I've not seen her before.

I think she's a teenager, fresh out of school.
This time last year she was acting the fool

on the school's corridors and on Instagram
but one year later she's pushing a pram.

A low life waster lives in Flat number six.
scrabbling around for his daily fix.

His face is drawn and his hair is long.
His life's a mess as it's all gone wrong.

He made a mistake! He joined the wrong crowd.
So there's more life now in the Turin shroud.

An air hostess lives in Flat number eight,
sharing her space with her lifelong mate.

Is she renting that apartment or is it hers,
bought from the profits of economy fares?

She leaves her flat in the middle of the night,
driving to the airport to catch her flight.

A separated girl lives in Flat number ten,
a pleasant young lady, with a boy called Ben.

She works so hard to provide for her son,
aided and abetted by her babysitting Mum.

Her husband's disappeared, as he wants to be single,
sampling the nightlife, a dance and a mingle.

Flat number twelve was always empty.

A recovering alcoholic lives in Flat 14,
looking like Rudolph, if you know what I mean.

I sometimes see him with a brown paper bag,
hobbling along whilst dragging on a fag.

I can see his vodka sticking out of the top,
bought from his dole from the corner shop.

A young executive lives in Flat 16,
driving a convertible, its bodywork pristine.

A supermodel girl often knocks on his door,
looking like she's launching Christian Dior.

'Some guys have all the luck,' I say to myself,
'Lots of us are fussy and end up on the shelf.'

And there's little old me, in Flat 18;
a scratched vinyl record and a tarnished dream.

My pocket's full of debts and lessons to be learned.
But who's responsible? The jury have adjourned.

I no longer reside in my rented abode,
in 'St Michael's View' - the name of that road.

My money and houses they vanished in a tryst,
devoured by a melancholy, monstrous mist.

'Guilty!' the judge shouts, banging his hammer.
'Your downfall's simple, it's your serious stammer!'

But whether I'm unhappy or I'm having a ball,
I'll remember the words on a plaque on my wall:

'Rejoice in what you have...'

Cherished number plates

Said NG 20 to FT 7
'Do you like my Mercedes?
It's the closest thing to heaven!'

Said KT 1 to FG 2
'I love my new Range rover,
it's all brand new.'

Said JKL 3 to TR 15
'Do you like my new Audi?
It drives like a dream!'

Said TW 9 to BP 8
'I'm in love with my Rolls,
and its cherished number plate.'

Sad ain't it?

A walk along a sandy shore.

How many pebbles lie on a crowded beach,
scattered like seeds from giants' hands?

Faded by centuries of sun beam bleach,
smoothed by rasping sands.

Millions and thousands and hundreds of stones,
older than the Book of Kells.

Nestled between seaweed and bones
and abandoned sea snail shells.

Wandering along that deserted shore,
a stranger walks his hound.

A hermit crab shelters, under a door.
A haven he has found.

Where's that door from? I wonder,
its paint all cracked and weathered.

A piece of sunken ship asunder
or an ogre's belt all leathered?

Teenage lovers' arms embrace
as they snatch a memorable kiss.

Stroking the rocks of a tall cliff face,
all happiness, love and bliss.

A hungry seagull swoops down low,
performing a high-pitched song.

And a ghostly wind doth hover and blow
pushing some children along.

An old mariner shines a midnight light
at a mermaid's silver scales.

Into the depths doth she dive from sight,
thrashing her slender tails.

She only appears at the sunrise hour
on ONE secret day a year.

She has mystical messages for all mankind
but nobody's there to hear.

The drifter

There he is, the drifter,
strutting around in those faded jeans.
A loser, a loner, a society misfit,
aimlessly wandering around our town.

He's 'stealing' a charity bag from a doorstep.
A new winter's wardrobe, perhaps?

He's picking up discarded cigarette ends
and lighting them up near the flats.

He's dragging a comb through his silver hair,
coated with oil, dirt and grease.

He's resting his bruised and battered body
on a bench for a few minutes' peace.

There he is, the drifter,
strutting around in those faded jeans.
A loser, a loner, a society misfit,
aimlessly wandering around our town.

He's enduring a barrage of barbarous insults,
from a shopkeeper who's yelling 'Get lost!'

He's staring at the face of Lewis' Snow Queen,
her words a threatening frost.

He's strolling down a crowded street,
counting concrete pavement cracks.

He's noticing people's silent stares,
as they turn their ignorant backs.

There he is, the drifter,
strutting around in those faded jeans.
A loser, a loner, a society misfit,
aimlessly wandering around our town.

He's whispering his tragic tales of life,
of horrors and unspeakable woe.

But everybody's rushing. They turn away
as nobody wants to know.

Online dating!

Everybody's visiting, looking for love.
Praying to their guardian angels above.

Casting their eyes on strangers' faces
in IPhone selfies of people and places.

Bruised and battered, unlucky in love.
Searching for Aphrodite's dove.

Trawling through plethoras of dull profiles,
of potential matches across the miles.

'Unluckyinlove' is a strange user name.
He wonders why but he's obviously to blame.

He's fifty now and still lives with his mother.
He had a girlfriend once but he'll never find another.

Tinsel15's a forty something divorcee.
She' got a teenage son and a toddler on her knee.

She's looking for a fella up to twenty-nine.
I think she typed her profile after copious wine.

Sporty31's a successful businessman.
His Ferrari's brand new but is it all a sham?

His profile's fake tan, all muscles and charms.
But he'll attract a bimbo, who'll hang from his arms.

Sparkle45 has travelled the earth,
exploring the planet's length and girth.

Her latest collection's another major city
graced with her presence – oh so pretty!

She's posting her photographs on this site.
Another expedition and a cruise and a flight.

A rocket to Jupiter's in the pipeline
and a tour of craters on Planet 69.

But now she's older and yearns to settle down.
Her parents' questions are causing her a frown.

They'd love a grandchild but they'll have to wait.
Because Sparkle45 has left it too late…

A whispering wind

A whispering wind speaks to me,
guiding me up a carriage.
A welcome break, an invisible friend,
pushing us into those seats.

You're pretty I know but filled with doubts.
Oh that troublesome road to love!
We share our tales of treading the earth,
as despair breeds lessons for life.

Two reserved seats for a long journey.
Two people just chatting away.
Two lonely hearts beating in temples
as Sirens sing their songs.

Angels gather as we talk,
binding us together.
Common ground is then discovered.
A never-ending chapter.

Funny how we both sat in those seats,
attracted like iron and magnet.
Chatting and chuckling all the way home.
Two spiritual beings living as one.

We said our goodbyes at that station
as the Virgin snake slithered away.
But I'll seize this moment just one more time.
For those whispering winds did mumble:

Rejoice oh kindred spirits!
Rejoice oh interlocked souls!
Rejoice oh happy hearts!
For you two shall meet again…

Kelda, the girl on the train
11th November 2015

Your country needs YOU!

'Your country needs you!' said the poster.
Just a piece of cardboard hanging on a wall.

Harry Malone marched past with his friends.
The long, and the short and the tall.

'Shall we join up and fight for our King?'
asked Harry, to his patriotic pals.

'If we can wear soldiers' uniforms,
we'll be chased around by gals.'

One by one, they scrawled their names,
signing their lives away.

Ink flowed through that golden nib,
on that fateful, life changing day.

The pals did train, at Salisbury plain,
over downs and English moors.

Battered by biting winds and rains
and Sergeant Majors' roars.

Harry did meet a beautiful girl.
His uniform did the trick.

A striking lass called Charlotte Brown,
with long, blonde hair so thick.

'Marry me please, when you come back home,'
said Charlotte, stealing a kiss.

'Of course I will,' said her handsome beloved.
'My heart, well it bursts with bliss.'

She handed her lover a lock of hair,
encased in a golden charm.

'Tuck me away in your pocket,' she said.
'I will keep you away from harm.'

Weeks passed by and Harry and pals
sailed on a boat to France.

His fiancée's voice and stunning face
performed a cinema dance.

Harry waited in his muddy trench
for his Captain's whistle to blow.

'Fix your bayonets!' a voice cried out.
'Fritz deserves a show!'

A piercing pitch punched the air -
a shrill but innocent sound.

And Harry's battalion went 'over the top'
by their generals' orders bound.

Harry and pals formed a line,
advancing through the mud.

Machine guns rattled and shrapnel flew.
And the earth was bathed in blood.

Harry clutched his golden charm,
housing his sweetheart's hair;

as he marched towards those Maxim guns
and into the devil's lair.

Three hot bullets strayed and sizzled
pounding Harry's chest.

And a soldier died for England
with his pals, who were the best.

Charlotte's hair is buried now,
deep under a farmer's field.

Safely hidden in her lover's pocket
but one day the earth shall yield.

Private Malone will be found one day,
along with his lover's charm.

Still together in that blood soaked field
on a peaceful Belgian farm.

Lest we forget...

Mr Conlon

Today I played the organ at Mr Conlon's funeral.
'Who's he?' I hear you whisper, narrowing eyes.
The old head teacher of my junior school.
A gentleman and a scholar.

You could say he existed in another age.
When teachers taught children the 'proper' way.
'Tempus Fugit' a long case ticks and tocks.
But memories are engraved like letters in stone:

Bernard Conlon:

Shy motivator.
Future creator.
Runt believer.
Dream conceiver.
Unique educator.

I stammered. I spluttered. I stuttered.
'Believe in yourself, Mr Delaney!'

'How?'

I stammered. I spluttered. I stuttered.
'You can do it, Mr Delaney!'

'Sure?'

I stammered. I spluttered. I stuttered.
'You CAN be a teacher – I know you can!'

'I doubt it!'

I stammered. I spluttered. I stuttered.
'It will all fall into place, Mr Delaney!'

And do you know what?
It did.

Bernard Conlon.
Talent spotter.

And all those dedicated teachers out there.
Talent spotters and dream makers and underdog believers and superhero motivators!

Better than Simon Cowell x

Mr Bernard Conlon

25th April 1930 – 4th October 2015

Window of appearances

Deep lines and wrinkles forged into her face.
A sun bleached photograph of a girl so chaste.

A chance encounter and love's misplaced.
And a spiral staircase to wild, withered waste.

Love's young dream nets an innocent teen.
A 'Jack the lad' but handsome and keen.

A beautiful waif courts celebrity's scene.
Destined for paths all miserable and mean.

A husband famous and loaded with money.
Respected reputations and an outlook sunny.

A secret mistress and a Playboy bunny.
And a web of deceit like sour tasting honey.

A tragic triangle of blood, sweat and tears.
And members of parliament and respected Peers.

Orchestral instruments playing unresolved fears.
Ignored and abandoned like Mediaeval Seers.

Three little children locked in barbaric cages.
Mummy and Daddy just turning the pages.

Acting their tragedy on theatrical stages.
An ancient story from prehistoric ages.

A tabloid newspaper's headline's uncovered.
The audience gasps as a secret's discovered.

A mountain of evidence is quickly recovered.
And a helpless lamb is nourished and mothered.

An unexploded bomb goes 'bang' in the beams.
Three peoples' hearts are ripped at the seams.

Life delivers nightmares not sugary dreams.
And three little children wonder what it all means…

One, two, three four five.

One, two, three four five.
Once I saw my Susan jive.

Six, seven, eight, nine, ten.
Then I let her go again.

Why did you let her go?
I was young and didn't know.

What memory remains?
Susan's woeful 'Don't leave!' pains.

Life's like following a football team.

A revolting river, a lethargic lake,
a heavily polluted mere.

Muddy water, once it's settled,
becomes a crystal clear.

Raging warriors invade our heads,
swords and shields a wielding.

Angelic choirs from a heavenly place
sing psalms and songs of healing.

Wicked wizards and wild, withered warlocks
conjure the pyres of hell.

And witches dance at unearthly hours,
in an ancient, woodland dell.

Guardian angels rest on shoulders,
pointing towards a light.

Saints and Sages, old and new,
their words a fresh insight.

Bruised and battered minds march on.
We're blood soaked battlefields.

Tidal waves of fictitious feelings
and a collection of cinema reels.

Multitudes of thoughts fly around,
a swarm of wasps and bees.

Buzzing in sunshine but silent in storms,
a forest of ancient sycamore trees.

Depressing lows to ecstatic highs.
Life's like following a football team.

You're designed to be happy ALL of the time
but alas, an impossible dream?

Megan and her mummy.

This reception class is silent.
Everybody has gone home.
They're only four and five years old.
All excited about Father Christmas.

Freya's picked up by her mummy.
Jake's picked up by his daddy.
Isabella's picked up by her grandad.
Oliver's picked up by his nanny.

Off they go to the park.
Off they go to the shops.
Off they go to the library.
Off they go back home.

Megan hasn't gone home.
She's still waiting for her mummy.
She's drawing a picture with Miss Harvey.
Minutes pass.

She's chatting to Miss Harvey.
Minutes pass.

She's giggling with Miss Harvey.
Minutes pass.

'I'm not in tomorrow, Megan!' I say,
pulling a silly, sad face.

'Aww,' Megan says, giving me a hug.

Megan's mummy finally arrives.
She's always incredibly late.
She's opened a box of excuses.
'Oh the traffic!'
'That stupid bus!'
'I lost my keys!'
'That silly school car park!'
'Somebody blocked me in!'

But everybody else is on time.
Every day.
They're distraught if they're late.
Except Megan's mummy.
She's *always* late.

She arrives with two social workers.
They sit around a table.
Miss Harvey disappears.
Everybody chats.
Megan's mummy says something.
Megan starts to cry.
Soon, her crying is long, deep sobbing.

I leave the classroom.
I start to make comparisons...

I wonder about Megan.
I wonder about her mummy.
I wonder about all the other children.

My heart grows heavy.

Tears invade my eyes.

I wonder about Megan.
I wonder about her mummy.
I wonder about all the other children.

But most of all, I wonder about Megan.
I wonder about her tainted young journey.
Her road's all narrow and twisted already.
And she's only four or five years old.
And merciless brambles strangle her heart.

But...

I hope happiness follows her footsteps.
I hope her heart's bathed in love.
I hope God strengthens this little girl's spirit
and she's a tower of strength for all to see!

But I will always wonder...

His life a different story?

He aimlessly wanders around the town,
a shadow of his former self.

A broken heart and a mangled mind.
He's definitely on the shelf.

His dreams have come and gone now.
He's sort of missed the bus.

He's playing his guitar on a lonely chair
on a carpet filled with dust.

His songs tell a story of falling in love,
a wife, three children and a house.

And a never-ending search in pubs and clubs,
looking for a suitable spouse.

He has no friends to share his woes,
his fears and tarnished dreams.

He has no coins in his moneybox.
Well, that's the way it seems.

He drifts around on the pavements,
stopping for occasional talks.

Bending the ears of his victims
encountered on his walks.

His clothes are old, weathered and worn.
So some turn their heads in shame.

Once upon a time, he was quite a catch,
a respected and popular name.

He looked for love in the usual places
but she never ever appeared.

He fell in love in those pubs and clubs
but now he's alone and weird.

If only he could have found his love,
all those many moons ago.

His life a different story, perhaps…
but we'll never ever know.

An unexploded silver bomb

In my nightmares appeared a harrowing image.
A haunting sight, punching at my eyes.
The drone of aeroplanes roared overhead.
A monotonous orchestral prelude
to a symphony of sorrowful songs
as the end of my comfortable world approached.

I heard its faint whistle as it descended.
Louder and louder its piercing pitch grew,
plunging and taunting through those thick clouds.

A bomb.
A huge silver bomb it was,
with red, monstrous eyes painted onto its nose.

Somebody had chalked
'Your life will never be the same again'
on the menace's smooth, silver sides.

The beast ripped through our roof and landed on my bed. It didn't explode immediately. It just sort of lay there on my blanket, those evil eyes staring out at me from the bottom of my bed.

A loud ticking sound escaped from its metal insides as it gently rocked to and fro, to and fro.

I had a feeling this would happen to my family.
Let's just call it a child's instinct.
As I waited, trembling, it finally happened.

An enormous, life-changing explosion ripped through our beautiful house, spreading red-hot shrapnel through bricks, mortar, timber…
AND hearts, minds and souls:

Mummy plunged through the East wall towards 'The grass is greener on the other side!' Street.

Daddy's body was blown through the West wall towards 'Uncharted territory' Avenue and 'Lonely' Lane, a junction, the road to nowhere.

I crashed through the North Wall, along with my twin sister, still clutching Jack and Sally, our unharmed teddy bears.

My younger brother and sister crashed through the South Wall, still snoozing and snoring in their warm bunk beds.

I pulled open my eyes as Jasper; our spaniel licked my face, his raspy tongue all warm and loving. He knew - I could see it in his eyes.

Me and Isobel, my twin sister and Grace and Noah all lay in the garden, amongst a huge heap of twisting metal, smoking wood and rubble.

A photograph of our family lay at my feet, its frame all punched and broken, its glass smashed into a hundred sharp and jagged jigsaw pieces.
I heard a muffled voice calling our names.

'Are you there, my loves? Are you there?'

'Is that you, Mummy?' I asked.
'Is that you, Daddy?'

I picked up that punctured photograph, my white fingers trembling. Staring at the happy faces inside its frame, covered in sharp, silver shards, my eyes released two solitary tears.

And then and only then, I realised one thing:

My life,
Isobel's life,
Grace's life,
Noah's life,
Mummy's life,
Daddy's life
would never ever be the same again…

You'll truly never part

When I release my final breath
and my spirit floats away,

my guardian angel will fly to you
and this is what she'll say:

'Rejoice! Rejoice! For he is gone
to the place where he belongs!

A realm of trumpet fanfares
and golden angel throngs!

Saints and sages welcome him
and Kings and ancient Queens.

He's promising still to speak to you
in whispers, visions and dreams.

Do not shed your earthly tears.
Do not feed your heavy heart.

He's vanished from your sight for now.
But you'll truly NEVER PART!

'I was just scared!'

'What on earth's SHE doing with HIM?'

'I don't know!'

'She must be easily pleased!'

'I suppose so!'

'I mean, hasn't she ever noticed me?'

'I doubt it!'

'Well what's so special about him?'

'How should I know?'

'He's a first class geek; it's obvious!'

'Have you ever even talked to her?'

'Err, no I, err, you know, was getting round to it.'

'Well that guy over there did get round to it!'

'I know and now he's Simone's boyfriend. And she's gorgeous!'

'Yes and you're on your own!'

'Stop laughing!'

'Sorry, I can't help it!'

'I'm on a downer now!'

'Well you should have asked her out first!'

'I know, but I was scared.'

'Scared of what?'

'Oh I don't know, just scared, that's all!'

'That she'd say 'Get lost' when you asked her?'

'Err, yes I suppose so!'

'Well that guy over there wasn't scared. He just went for it and now he's got the prettiest girl in the college hanging off his arm.'

'Alright, don't rub it in!'

'It's true, so in future, remember only this:

Face your fears...and do it anyway!

My spirit's return

If my sunken spirit returns to this planet,
on a distant, future day,
a handful of wishes I will bring
and this is what I'll say:

Can my soul be bathed in love
as a cactus soaks up rain?
Can my tongue be a very good friend
not a symbol of pity and shame?

Can my heart be light and free
like flowers basking in sun?
Can my paths be straight and narrow,
not a meandering marathon run?

If the answer is yes, then I'll be happy...

Selected songs from my musicals

Emily

(from 'Christmas at Holly Lodge' 1997)

I am sitting in a deep and dirty trench,
talking of what they will be doing back home.

I long to see my homeland again,
I'm petrified but it don't show.

It's my duty to inform you,
that your father fell today.

Please say a prayer for him
in the chapel if you may.

I have lost all my school friends,
I've come close to death myself.
Heaven's staircase must be crowded today.

Emily, I hold your letter in my hand.
Please believe, that I'll come back home.
When the war is over, I will marry you, my dear.
Still the faintest fragrance lingers on.

I am listening to the shells,
wishing I could hear wedding bells.
Closing my eyes I picture us on our wedding day.

Save this land

(from 'My grandad's field' 1996)

There are echoes in the valleys,
whispers in the deep.
There's a thousand ghostly voices,
the spirits of the trees.
There's a voice that cries from heaven,
that's telling me to save this land.

There's a feeling in the forest.
Excitement in the skies.
There's a thousand heavenly angels,
humans in disguise.
There's a voice that cries from heaven,
that's telling me to save this land.

I can do nothing, without the help of God
but surely, God is on my side.
I must preserve our heritage for future generations.
Though stormy waters, I will turn the tide.

The song of the tree

(from 'My grandad's field')

If you knew what I'd been through, you'd care.
If you knew what I had seen, you'd change your mind.
If you could see my memories inside.
To the homeless, I'm a shelter, I am wise.

I've been standing for a thousand years.
I have braved the fiercest storms, the wind and rain.
I remember my battles with the lightning.
I could write a history book about the Vikings.

But my biggest test is now.
I'm no match for the machines of modern man,
Who believe, then deceive, the trees.
All my wisdom will be gone
and a secret of the world will fly away
and the children, of the world, will:

Never see my shadow on a hot summer's day.
Never hide behind me when they're playing a game.
Never climb my branches during curious play.
Mankind must change. I hope it's not too late…

My new world

(from 'Dr Jekyll and Mr Hyde' 1994)

Close your eyes, sit upon a star.
I'm surprised to see you weeping.

Float away, into the night sky.
Come up and see how I'm keeping.

Let me take you to my world tonight.
Let us celebrate my life.

Gentle breeze, lifting fallen seeds.
Nature's way of reproducing.

Autumn leaves, stripped of all their leaves.
Springtime's transformation, gleaming.

Like the mysteries of the universe,
I have simply travelled on…

to my new world.

For you I'd give up everything

(From 'Dr Jekyll and Mr Hyde')

For you I'd give up everything.
For you I'd fight a thousand Kings.
For you I'd capture raindrops
and change them into diamonds
and polish them until I see your face.

For you I'd even sell my soul.
For you I'd wait 'till I was old.
For you I'd capture eagles
and learn their flying secrets,
then we could fly together in the sky.

Like a very special treasured memory,
there are certain things that stand the test of time.
Proving that you love me is no reason,
I am sure of you, I have received a sign.

London town

(from 'Mister Scrooge' 1998)

We are at work in the market,
selling our wares on the street!
Lovely fresh flowers and juicy fresh fruit,
selling our goods to delight.
What can you buy in the market?
Linen, tobacco and wine.
In fact you can buy anything you want,
from early 'till half past five!

**London town at Christmas time
is full of joy and festive cheer.
Take your time to look around,
my friend, this market's very cheap.
Do you want to buy a present?
Do you want a glass of beer?
London town is so exciting,
as Christmas time draws near.**

Apples, oranges, two for a farthing!
Get your mistletoe here!
Cheap China plates and porcelain dolls!
It's the bargain of the year!
Mince pies! Mince pies! Get your mince pies!
Christmas trees only a shilling!
Christmas pudding, Christmas pudding!
Freshly baked today!

I am still here, so that's good...

'Imagination is everything. It is the preview of life's coming attractions...'

Albert Einstein
Legendary German physicist
1879 - 1955

'Chinese dragon fly swiftly,
over the hills in vain.
Watch and wonder where to go,
running in the rain.'

'To invent, you need a good imagination and a pile of junk!'

Thomas A Edison
Inventor of the electric light bulb
1847 - 1941

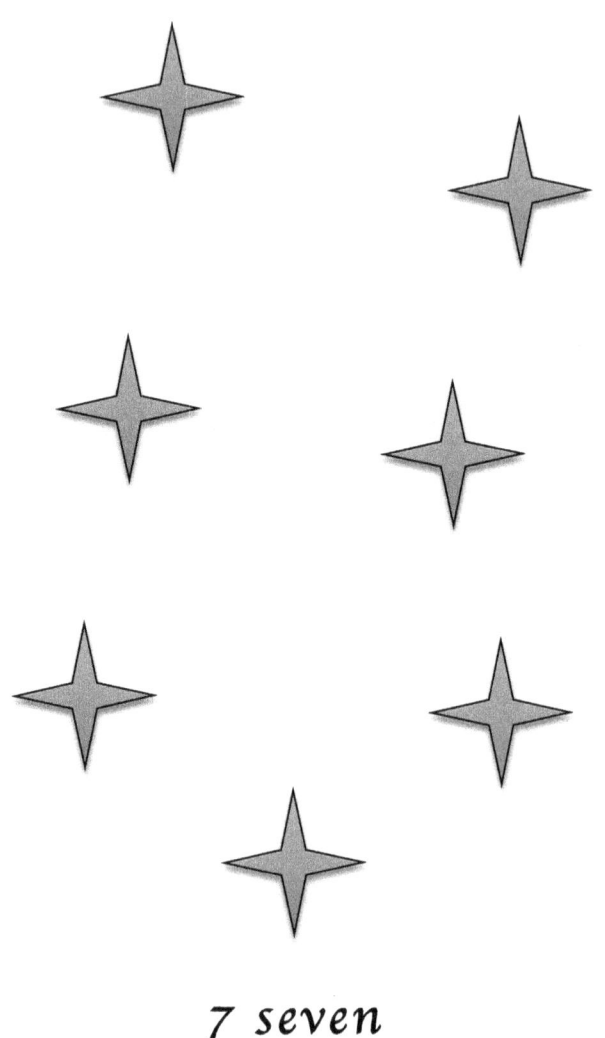

7 seven

DBM
(*Don't bore me!*)

555

La fin

Index of the '44'

A bird with a broken wing 28
A definition of clauses 46
A frog saw his love 62
A load of words 34
A serendipitous dog walk 35
A walk along a sandy shore 70
A whispering wind 76
An unexploded silver bomb 95
Cherished number plates 69

Father Michael's favourite dish 47
Four imaginary walls 25
His life a different story 93

I blame myself 64
I love your beautiful mind 49
I suppose I'll never know 39
'I was just scared!' 99

Johnny Johnson's Spitfire 37
Life is strange 24
Life's like following a football team 88

Megan and her mummy 90
Menagerie minds 44
Miss Campbell's sweet revenge 15
Mr Conlon 82
Mrs Flossop's date with destiny 52
My favourite trainers 11
My spirit's return 102
One, two, three, four, five 87
Online dating 74
Our children's beautiful toys 58
Our heads – a menagerie! 45
People 57

Ripples in a pond 30
Seven supermarket trolleys 18
St Michael's View 66
Thank you! 59
The door in the corner 26
The drifter 72
The invisible fisherman 21
The tragic and cruel life of a teabag 17
The staffroom of broken dreams 32
Two childhood jigsaws 13

Window of appearances 85
Why not? 41
You'll never truly part 98
Your country needs you! 78

There are NO poems left in this book!

Lightning Source UK Ltd.
Milton Keynes UK
UKOW05f2114110617
303133UK00001B/186/P

9 781786 976956